You Can't Eat Peanuts in Church

and Other Little-known Laws

You Can't Eat Peanuts
in Church
and Other Little-known
Laws

Written and Illustrated by
Barbara Seuling

Doubleday & Company, Inc., Garden City, New York

To Nancy and Sandy

Library of Congress Cataloging in Publication Data

Seuling, Barbara.
    You can't eat peanuts in church and other little-known laws.

    SUMMARY: A cartoon joke book presenting some unusual laws in effect at one time or another in the United States.
    1. Law—United States—Juvenile literature.
[1. Law.   2. Joke books]   I. Title.
KF387.S439   340'.0973
ISBN 0-385-01393-0 Trade
        0-385-01435-X Prebound
Library of Congress Catalog Card Number 74–19384

INTRODUCTION

American legislation is not unique in its peculiarities. In Cambodia, for instance, it was once against the law to insult a rice plant. In the time of Henry III of England, death was the penalty for "kyllnge, woundynge, or mamynge" a fairy. In the Soviet Union, a train coming upon a sleeping citizen was forced to stop and wait for him to finish his nap.

We must assume there is, or was, a good reason for all of these laws, although many of the reasons are lost in history and others we can only guess at from existing clues.

We know that religious beliefs account for some laws, modern as well as ancient. In Egypt, cats were once looked upon as gods, and killing one, even by accident, was punishable by death.

Despotic rulers, from time to time, created laws for their own protection, either physical or psychological. A man could be put to death in ancient Persia if, while tidying up, he accidentally sat on the king's throne. In third-century Rome, the Emperor Claudius tried to abolish by law the institution of marriage because he felt that married men made terrible soldiers, but a subversive named Valentine came along with an underground love-and-marriage movement and wrecked the plan.

Native custom or superstition was frequently woven into laws. In early times, people believed a man's soul lived in his shoes. Thus, shoes, or sandals, were considered sacred, and even used as legal tools. Casting one's sandal on a piece of land was equivalent to taking possession of it. The giving of a shoe to a new owner of a house by the former owner constituted a legal procedure and was as good as giving him the deed.

The Roman custom of breaking the wedding cake over the bride's head was more than just a tradition. By law, only children born of a bride who took part in this ceremony were later eligible to assume high offices in Roman life.

But before we laugh at the ancients, remember that it was only about a decade ago that men wearing long hair and women wearing pants were breaking the law in many states.

In our own country, the first laws were really carryovers from England. By today's standards some may seem unusually cruel and unfair, but for the time, they were models of progressive liberality. When the colonists here were demanding the death penalty for being "a stubborn and rebellious son" or for worshiping "any other God but the true God," tiny children were being hanged in England for stealing a few pennies or a loaf of bread. And while hanging, thought to be the most humane method of execution, was the standard death penalty in all the American colonies, England and other countries around the globe were still devising ingenious ways to maim, torture, and grotesquely kill offenders of the law, for crimes no more horrendous than thinking wicked thoughts.

The Puritan fathers, responsible for the earliest laws governing life, liberty, and the pursuit of happiness in the American colonies, used the Bible as the basis for legislation. There was no flexibility. Their interpretation of the Bible was strict; and so were the laws. Alas, they did not know that morality cannot be legislated.

We may think that Puritan ethics and these old laws got buried in the past along with muskets and witchcraft trials, but it is not true. Many old laws were never taken off the books. Again and again throughout our history laws were enacted when needed as the country expanded. But times changed faster than the laws and one day it was too late. Some old laws were so quaint that to tamper with them seemed like a travesty. Others remained because there was simply not enough time to go through all the legal steps to uncover and remove them. And so they remained, a monument to legal history, rather than as rules to be enforced. As for Puritan ethics, it was as recent as 1925 that a man was put on trial for teaching man's evolution from apes, which was against the strict biblical interpretation of man's creation . . . and against the law of the state of Tennessee.

Some legislation simply got into the hands of over-eager draftsmen, who puffed up their roles a bit when they took a two-bit law and made it sound like a ten-dollar one. Once in "legalese" instead of plain English, laws were difficult to read, harder to interpret, and often misleading. Someone once amusingly wrote:

> *"I'm the Parliamentary Draftsman,*
> *I compose the country's laws,*
> *And of half the litigation*
> *I'm undoubtedly the cause."*

What makes some American laws seem so ridiculous and different in character from strange laws of other countries, is their superspecific nature. Every offense imaginable seems to be described in detail by statute. In the criminal codes of the fifty states, there is enough information for a complete guidebook on how to commit crimes. Like the admonishment "Don't put beans up your nose," such laws might possibly act more as suggestions than as discouragements. A law on the books of several states, written some years ago when most women wore hats, goes into fine detail about the legal length of hatpins, down to the precise half inch of proper exposure. A more general law about sharp objects in public might have been more logical, and quite a bit safer, than what is still on the books as a hatpin law.

There are other reasons too for strange laws. Occasionally states of emergency or temporary public nuisances are the cause for new laws, but the laws remain even after the crises pass. Or old laws are "modernized." This often means a substitution of words, like "car" for "buggy," but in essence, the laws remain just as peculiar as ever. It has also been known to happen that members of legislative bodies, looking for something worthwhile to do after all other business has been delegated to subcommittees, will pass a law or two. And then there are the outright bloopers—for example, the Illinois state motor vehicle law which states that it is illegal "to move or attempt to move a motor vehicle." If that law were taken literally, no driver would be able to drive his own car.

Despite our efforts, it is doubtful that we will ever solve the mystery of some remaining strange laws. So we will have to go on wondering why it was illegal in the old days to wipe dishes, or to have an aerial on your radio, and even how a monkey could be brought to trial and convicted!

No doubt some of the laws in this book are no longer alive. Laws are repealed and enacted every day. These are just some of the laughable laws that were written at one time in history. As a matter of fact, based on past experience, I wouldn't be surprised if someone were whipping up a brand-new freaky law right now!

The law requires that between March 1 and October 20, residents of Nottingham, Maryland, must let their hogs roam free.

Hunting elk on Main Street in Ouray, California, is prohibited by law.

An early-twentieth-century law passed in Meridian, Mississippi, forbids businessmen to beat drums during a lunchtime stroll.

Lest little boys of Ashland, Wisconsin, grow up to be gamblers, a law has been enacted making it illegal to play marbles for keeps.

In Star, Mississippi, it is a punishable offense to ridicule public architecture.

A federal law prohibits women from tagging along with American troops as laundresses.

To take a bath in Boston, you must have a doctor's written prescription.

Wearing suspenders is illegal in Nogales, Arizona.

Movies containing prizefighting scenes cannot be shown in Wichita, Kansas.

In South Dakota, an eighty-year-old woman cannot stop on the street to talk to a young married man.

It is illegal to own both a cat and a bird in Reed City, Michigan.

A Louisiana law upholds your right to grow as tall as you like.

Barbers in Hawaii are not permitted to lather the chins of their customers with a shaving brush.

Spitting against the wind in Sault Sainte Marie, Michigan, is unlawful.

In Wyoming, it is illegal to take a picture of a rabbit during January, February, March, or April—unless you have a license.

Federal law maintains that no living person can be portrayed on United States paper currency.

A California law makes it illegal for a woman to go for a drive in her housecoat.

It is illegal to walk through the streets of Maine with your shoelaces undone.

In St. Louis, Missouri, it is against the law to let rubbish collect on your roof.

Public checker-playing is against the law in La Crosse, Wisconsin.

The law prohibits females from wearing any kind of transparent apparel in Providence, Rhode Island.

Prisoners in Charleston, South Carolina, were once charged a dollar fare for the ride to jail.

Singing out of tune in North Carolina is against the law.

In Whitehall, Montana, it is unlawful to drive a truck or car with ice picks fitted to the wheels.

In Terre Haute, Indiana, women's dresses may be no more than two inches above the ankle.

In a case in which a drunk sued for damages when he tripped on a broken sidewalk, a California judge decided that "a drunken man has as good a right to a perfect sidewalk as a sober man, and he needs one a good deal more."

A woman cannot take a bath in a business office in Carmel, California.

An old law in Brainerd, Minnesota, orders that every male must grow a beard.

It is illegal to shoot open a can of food in Spades, Indiana.

Picking feathers from a live goose in California is illegal.

Several states—California, Oklahoma, Idaho, and North Dakota—prohibit the trapping of birds in cemeteries.

In Natoma, Kansas, it is illegal to practice knife throwing at someone wearing a striped suit.

The laws of Portland, Maine, do not allow one to tickle a girl under the chin with a feather duster.

Carrying a lunch bucket on the street in Riverside, California, is against the law.

It is illegal to slide on the ice on the sidewalks of Wilmington, Delaware.

In Kentucky, a man may not marry his wife's grandmother.

Anyone over the age of eighty-eight in Idaho Falls, Idaho, is not permitted to ride a motorcycle.

In Hammond, Indiana, it is illegal to throw watermelon seeds on the sidewalk.

During bank holidays in Michigan, the size of wheatcakes is regulated by law.

It is unlawful to ride a tricycle on the sidewalk in Moscow, Idaho.

It was once illegal in Boston, Massachusetts, to own a dog more than ten inches high.

The Wisconsin legislature passed a law ordering that with each meal sold in the state for twenty-five cents or more, a minimum of two thirds of an ounce of cheese must be served.

In Ziegler, Illinois, a law provides that the first four firemen to show up at a fire will be paid for their services.

A hotel owner in Boston, Massachusetts, is required by law to put up and bed down a guest's horse.

Every man in Phoenix, Arizona, must wear pants when he comes to town.

You can attach a horn to your bicycle in New Mexico only if it produces a harmonious sound.

According to a health ordinance in Riverside, California, kissing on the lips is against the law unless both parties first wipe their lips with carbolized rose water.

A New York judge ruled that if two women behind you in a movie house are discussing the probable outcome of a film, you can give them a Bronx cheer.

It is unlawful to drink water or milk on a train in North Carolina.

In Massachusetts, it is an infraction of the law to lounge around on bakery shelves.

According to an old law of Truro, Massachusetts, a young man could not get married until he had killed either six blackbirds or three crows.

It is unlawful to hold frog-jumping contests in Boston night clubs.

It is against the law to drive camels along Nevada's main highways.

Employees in Concord, New Hampshire, are not permitted to work in bare feet.

A Kentucky statute reads:
"No female shall appear in a bathing suit on any highway within this state unless she is escorted by at least two officers or unless she be armed with a club."
A subsequent amendment to the original statute reads:
"The provisions of this statute shall not apply to females weighing less than 90 pounds nor exceeding 200 pounds; nor shall it apply to female horses."

New Jersey law provides that no one shall delay or detain a homing pigeon.

It is an unlawful offense to criticize the city of Auchula, Florida.

It is illegal to set a trap for a mouse in California without a hunting license.

In Hawaii, it is illegal to insert pennies in your ears.

Idaho law makes it illegal to give your sweetheart a box of candy weighing less than fifty pounds.

In Massachusetts, digging up the state flower, the Mayflower, is punishable by a fifty-dollar fine. For digging in disguise, however, the fine is one hundred dollars.

A bill collector in Massachusetts is not permitted to dress in "unusual or striking costumes."

In Kentucky, you may not shoot clay pigeons during the breeding season.

All bicycles in Pueblo, Colorado, must carry gongs.

Taking a fish off another person's hook is against the law in Tennessee.

Calling to someone on the street is against the law in Valentine, Nebraska.

Two people are not permitted on a bicycle at the same time in Muskegan, Michigan.

You are not permitted to swim on dry land in Santa Ana, California.

Setting fire to a mule is prohibited in Maine.

It is a crime in several states to dance to "The Star-Spangled Banner."

An old law of South Foster, Rhode Island, declares that if a dentist makes a mistake and pulls a wrong tooth, the penalty is to have a corresponding tooth extracted from his mouth by the village blacksmith.

In Alabama, books about outlaws are banned.

In Florida, if a voter remains in an election booth for more than five minutes, he can be fined and sent to prison.

In Gary, Indiana, it is illegal to attend the theater within four hours of eating garlic.

In Tahoe City, California, cowbells may not be worn by horses.

It is illegal for a dog to come within ten feet of a fire hydrant in Sheridan, Wyoming.

It is unlawful to whistle on Sunday in Louisiana.

A man in Alabama may lawfully discipline his wife by using "a stick no larger than the thumb."

In Denver, Colorado, the law insists that dog-catchers notify dogs of impounding by posting a notice on a tree in the park.

It is a crime to kick a mule in Arizona.

In New York, it is unlawful to disturb the occupant of a house by ringing the doorbell.

In Ohio, the victim of a lynch mob is entitled to recover a sum of up to five hundred dollars from the county in which the assault took place.

In Dunlap, West Virginia, it is illegal to tear up a marriage certificate.

Lions are not permitted to run wild on the streets of Alderson, West Virginia.

In Connecticut, the law states that if you are a beaver, you have a legal right to build a dam.

It is illegal for a chicken to cross the road in Quitman, Georgia.

North Dakota railroad engineers may not take their trains home with them at night unless they carry a full crew.

It is illegal for a dead juror to serve on a jury, according to Oregon law.

A married couple in Michigan must live together or be imprisoned.

It is illegal to put tomatoes in clam chowder in Massachusetts.

A Belvedere, California, ordinance was written: "No dog shall be in public without its master on a leash."

You may not sleep in a refrigerator in Pittsburgh, Pennsylvania.

The law of St. Joseph, Missouri, states that firemen cannot cavort about in their undershirts.

All citizens of South Carolina are required to carry guns with them to church on Sunday.

In Lang, Kansas, you cannot drive a mule down Main Street in the month of August without wearing a straw hat.

In Paulding, Ohio, it is legally proper for a policeman to bite a barking dog to quiet him.

In Kansas, it is a crime to exhibit the eating of snakes.

In Poplar Bluff, Missouri, shaving in the daytime is unlawful.

In Marblehead, Massachusetts, it is illegal to cross the street on Sunday unless it is absolutely necessary.

Waiters in Topeka, Kansas, may not serve wine in teacups.

In Idaho, you cannot fish for trout from the back of a giraffe.

In Glendale, Arizona, it is against the law to back up your car.

In Nebraska, sneezing in public is prohibited by law.

According to the law, you can only "act in an obnoxious manner on the campus of a girls' school" in the state of South Carolina if you have the principal's permission.

In San Francisco, you are forbidden by law to spit on your laundry.

On the sidewalks of Hiawatha, Kansas, firemen going to and coming from a fire on their bicycles have the right of way.

In Idaho, you cannot buy a chicken after dark without the sheriff's permission.

An old Boston law prohibited citizens from taking more than one bath each week.

If a Michigan woman leaves her husband, then he is entitled to take possession of all her clothing.

In Nashville, Tennessee, only janitors are allowed by law to live in penthouses.

In Massachusetts there was a law forbidding the showing of movies which lasted longer than twenty minutes.

A man can be sent to the penitentiary in Texas if he is found carrying a pair of pliers.

The law prohibits unrestrained giggling in Helena, Montana.

Fiddle playing is outlawed in Boston.

A kiss can last no longer than one second in Halethorpe, Maryland.

It is illegal to eat peanuts in church in Massachusetts.

It is illegal to throw shoes at the bridal couple in a Colorado wedding.

In Rochester, Michigan, you must have your bathing suit inspected by the police before bathing in public.

In Osceola, Michigan, if a bicyclist wants to pass a horse-drawn vehicle, he must get the permission of the driver first.

In Baltimore, Maryland, it is against the law to mistreat an oyster.

Fire trucks and ambulances cannot go faster than twenty miles per hour in Port Huron, Michigan.

In Waterloo, Nebraska, barbers are not allowed to eat onions during working hours.

A sea captain in colonial Boston had to spend two hours in the stocks for kissing his wife in public on Sunday after returning from three years at sea.

In the state of Illinois an animal can be sent to jail.

In Los Angeles, California, you cannot use the U.S. mails to complain about cockroaches in your hotel room.

In Topeka, Kansas, it is illegal to worry a squirrel.

In Oklahoma, eavesdropping is illegal.

An old law in Arkansas states that an automobile must be preceded by a man carrying a red flag.

An ordinance in Bristow, Oklahoma, requires public eating houses to serve each customer one peanut in the shell with every glass of water.

In Indiana a mustache is illegal on anyone who "habitually kisses human beings."

A girl in Dyersburg, Tennessee, cannot phone a man for a date, under penalty of law.

In Johnson City, New York, a person may not wander from the right to the left side of the sidewalk.

It is illegal for monkeys to ride buses in San Antonio, Texas.

In New York City it is against the law to enter or leave a city park wearing a flower.

In Salem, Massachusetts, the law requires an innkeeper to provide each overnight guest with a clean nightshirt.

Arkansas state law prohibits the blindfolding of cows on public highways.

In seventeenth-century Connecticut, a person could receive the death penalty for disobeying a parent.

In Georgia, a dentist can be charged with a misdemeanor if found guilty of cruelty.

Sheep are allowed to graze on Baldwin Hill in Los Angeles as long as they leave two inches of grass.

In Kentucky a wife must have her husband's permission to move the furniture in her house.

In Illinois, using dynamite to catch fish is not allowed.

You are prohibited from punching a bull in the nose in Washington, D.C.

An ordinance of Pocatello, Idaho, makes it illegal to look gloomy.

An Oklahoma statute of 1931 proclaimed that a steamboat captain could be held guilty of manslaughter if his boat blew up and killed anyone during a boat race.

Florida law requires that you wear clothing when you take a bath in a bathtub.

In California, it is illegal to peel an orange in your hotel room.

In Los Angeles, it is unlawful to shoot at a person stealing a bicycle.

You cannot fly a kite in the city of Washington, D.C.

An animal on the street after dark in Berea, Ohio, must display a red tail light.

The law in Minneapolis, Minnesota, prohibits driving red automobiles.

It is illegal to climb up a building in New Mexico to get a free view of a ball game.

In Detroit, Michigan, it is unlawful to sell confetti.

Women may not shine their shoes on Saturday in Marshall, Minnesota.

An old Hollywood, California, ordinance forbids driving more than two thousand sheep down Hollywood Boulevard at one time.

In Klamath Falls, Oregon, it is illegal to kick the heads off snakes.

Anyone stealing citrus fruit in Yuma, Arizona, can legally be given castor oil as a punishment.

In the Pine Island District of Minnesota, a man must tip his hat when passing a cow.

A federal law of 1864 permits a woman to get a divorce if her husband is in the United States military service.

A Minnesota law requires that men's and women's underwear not be hung on the same clothesline at the same time.

In the state of Washington, it is illegal to hunt ducks from a rowboat unless you are upright and visible from the waist up.

The California penal code prohibits the shooting of any animal, except a whale, from an automobile.

It is illegal to lasso a fish in Knoxville, Tennessee.

Wearing a mask in Denver, Colorado, is forbidden by law.

It is illegal in Elkhart, Indiana, for a barber to threaten to cut off a child's ears.

In Michigan you may not hitch a crocodile to a fire hydrant.

The legal punishment in Minneapolis, Minnesota, for double-parking is being put on a chain gang and fed only bread and water.

In Kentucky, there is a law against sleeping in a restaurant.

A child under twelve in Blue Earth, Minnesota, must be accompanied by a parent when using the telephone.

A Michigan woman is not allowed to lift her skirt more than six inches to avoid mud puddles.

All fishermen in Maine are required by law to take off their hats to the game warden.

It is a capital offense in South Carolina to kill someone accidentally while attempting to commit suicide.

In Maine, buildings made of round logs are tax exempt.

The Halsey, Nebraska, town constable is required by law to remember his manners at all times.

In Hattiesburg, Mississippi, it is unlawful to milk another person's cow.

In Evansville, Indiana, hamburgers may not be sold on Sunday.

There must be a hitching post in front of every house in Omaha, Nebraska.

In West Virginia, you are not permitted to sneeze on a train.

It is unlawful to mistreat a rat in Denver, Colorado.

In Maine you cannot lead a bear around by a rope.

An old Georgia law requires a beach guard to wear a bright red bathing suit, and a harness around his neck attached to a 200-foot-long lifeline.

In Detroit, Michigan, you are not allowed to fall asleep in the bathtub.

Each fire company responding to a fire alarm in Marblehead, Massachusetts, is legally entitled to a three-gallon jug of rum.

The New York State Vehicle and Traffic Law states: "Two vehicles which are passing each other in opposite directions shall have the right of way."

In Mississippi, you can be arrested for soaping the railroad tracks.

In Connecticut, if a girl's mother forbids a suitor to see her daughter, the man cannot write love letters to the girl or he is breaking the law.

A city ordinance in Ontario, California, forbids roosters to crow within city limits.

Throwing rice at weddings is illegal in Chillicothe, Missouri.

A girl in Norfolk, Virginia, attending a public dance without wearing a corset is in violation of the law.

Anyone caught leaning against a public building in Clinton County, Ohio, can be fined.

In Stillwater, Missouri, it is illegal to have a pet bat.

If a person is caught stealing soap in Mohave County, Arizona, he must wash with it until it is all used up.

In St. Paul, Minnesota, you are not allowed to take pigs into public buildings.

Michigan law once required taking a census of bees every winter.

In New York City it is a violation of the law to carry a skeleton into a tenement house.

In Lexington, Kentucky, you are forbidden by law to carry ice cream cones in your pocket.

In Little Rock, Arkansas, it is unlawful to frighten a horse with a flying kite.

Mules are prohibited from going into saloons in Lourdsburg, New Mexico.

Bald men who visit beauty shops in New York City to have their hair regrown are breaking the law.

Dogs are not allowed to bark after 6 P.M. in Little Rock, Arkansas.

In Roderfield, West Virginia, only babies are allowed to ride in baby carriages.

A New York court decision reads: "A railway company which negligently throws a passenger from a crowded car on a trestle is held liable for injury to a relative who, in going to his rescue, falls through the trestle."

In Washington, D.C., a taxi must carry a broom and a shovel.

It is unlawful in Portland, Oregon, to wear roller skates in a public rest room.

Heels higher than 1½ inches are outlawed in Utah.

In Baltimore, Maryland, the sale of parrots is illegal.

The law of Barre, Vermont, requires that everyone must take a bath on Saturday night.

In Cleveland, Ohio, it is against the law for two men to drink from the same whisky bottle.

You are breaking the law if you allow your car to backfire in Rutland, Vermont.

In San Francisco you are not permitted to carry a basket suspended from a pole.

In Alabama, it is illegal to buy a sack of peanuts after sunset.

An old ordinance of New London, Connecticut, forbids an actress from appearing in public.

In Atlanta, Georgia, smelly persons are not allowed on streetcars.

If, in Connecticut, you fly an American flag which has lost one or more of its stars or stripes, you can be fined up to seven dollars.

In Gurnee, Illinois, a two-hundred-pound woman is not allowed to wear shorts when riding a horse.

It is illegal in Columbia, Tennessee, for a woman to walk down the street if she is not wearing a petticoat.

In Alabama the law prohibits putting salt on the railroad tracks.

In Owensboro, Kentucky, if a woman wants to buy a new hat, her husband must try it on first.

Motorists approaching the city of Tacoma, Washington, were once required to stop and phone ahead to the police chief to announce their arrival.

In Corinth, Mississippi, the sale of ice cream on Sunday is illegal.

A Virginia law makes it illegal to have a bathtub in one's house.

In New Orleans, a fire engine must stop for a red light, even if it is on its way to a fire.

It is actually illegal to speak English in Illinois. According to a revised statute of 1919, which author H. L. Mencken helped to establish, the official language of the state of Illinois is "American," which Mr. Mencken felt was distinctly different from English.

You are not allowed to draw funny faces on your window shades in Garfield County, Montana.

It is illegal to grow dandelions in Pueblo, Colorado.

In Minneapolis, Minnesota, it is illegal to install a bathtub in your home unless it has legs.

In Pennsylvania, the penalty for cursing is a forty-cent fine. However, if God is mentioned in the curse, the fine is sixty-seven cents.

An Indiana law requires that hotel bed sheets be at least ninety-nine inches long and eighty-one inches wide.

In Wichita, Kansas, it is illegal to carry a concealed bean snapper.

Frightening a baby is an infraction of the law in Molie, Missouri.

If you buy a can of snuff in Mississippi, you must stand at least an arm's length from the seller.

In Bellingham, Washington, a woman may not take more than three steps backward while dancing.

The law forbids women of Oxford, Ohio, from undressing in front of the photograph of a man.

In Durango, Colorado, it is illegal to swim in a pool or a river during the daytime.

In Cedar Rapids, Iowa, you are not permitted to kiss a stranger.

Oklahoma, a totally inland state, has a law against catching whales in its waters.

In Joliet, Illinois, women are not allowed to try on more than six dresses in one store.

Iowa women are not allowed to wear corsets. There were once even corset inspectors, whose duty it was to poke women in the ribs to see if they had them on.

Until this century, dachshunds could not be kept as pets in Massachusetts.

On Market Street in San Francisco, the law requires that elephants must be kept on a leash.

In Arkansas and South Carolina, it is illegal to file down a mule's teeth.

In Glendale, California, horror films can be shown only on Mondays, Tuesdays, and Wednesdays.

Punch and Judy puppets in Warren, Idaho, are required by law to wear American clothes.

It is illegal for a donkey to sleep in a bathtub in Brooklyn, New York.

Los Angeles bartenders cannot give pet animals away to their customers.

The Paiute Indians in California ban mothers-in-law from spending more than thirty days a year with their children.

In Nebraska, you may not picnic in the same place within a thirty-day period.

The law forbids loud talking at picnics in the state of Pennsylvania.

An Arkansas law prohibits setting up a lunch counter on Decoration Day within half a mile of the Confederate cemetery.

In San Jose, California, sleeping in your neighbor's outhouse without his permission is in violation of the law.

In New York, it is a misdemeanor to arrest a dead man for a debt.

It is illegal for bees to fly over the town of Kirkland, Illinois.

In Louisiana it is outside the law for a beauty operator to put cold cream or powder on a customer's feet.

In Cold Spring, Pennsylvania, liquor can only be sold to a married man if he has his wife's written permission.

In Muncie, Indiana, you cannot bring fishing tackle into a cemetery.

In Oxford, Ohio, patent leather shoes for women are not allowed. It was believed indecent to wear shoes that would reflect one's legs for all to see.

Every Pennsylvania innkeeper is required by law to provide good entertainment for his or her guests.

In Wichita, Kansas, a hobo cannot sleep in an empty boxcar unless he first obtains the permission of the president of the railroad company.

In Rumford, Maine, it is against the law to bite your landlord.

In Topeka, Kansas, it is illegal to have more than five cats in one household.

Colorado state law makes it illegal to watch a dogfight.

It is illegal in New York to play cards on a train.

In Saco, Missouri, hats which may frighten timid people are outlawed.

A man in an Erie, Pennsylvania, barbershop is not allowed to fall asleep while being shaved.

Bus companies in North Carolina have the legal right to provide free transportation to blind preachers.

In Kansas City, Missouri, children are prohibited by law from buying cap pistols. However, the law does not restrict them from buying shotguns.

In Philadelphia, wrestlers can be fined for throwing their opponents out of the ring during a match.

You are breaking the law if you tickle a girl in Norton, Virginia.

It is an infringement of the law in Alabama to wear a false mustache in church if it makes people laugh.

In Dunn, North Carolina, you are breaking the law if you snore and disturb your neighbor.

In Clawson City, Michigan, people may lawfully sleep with their pigs, cows, and chickens.

In San Francisco, you cannot legally buy a glass of milk. The law requires that all milk be sold in sealed glass bottles.

In Zion City, Illinois, it is illegal to make ugly faces at anyone.

It is unlawful to keep a prisoner in jail on Sunday in Kulpmont, Pennsylvania.

Indiana state law forbids roller-skating in-structors from leading their female students astray during lessons.

Driving your car down the street in Parsons, Kansas, without a horse hitched to it, is against the law.

In Chicago, anyone who drinks standing up is breaking the law.

According to Kentucky law, "burglary can only be committed in the night-time."

In Colorado, it is illegal to hunt ducks from an airplane.

In a Manville, New Jersey, public park, you are not allowed to feed whisky or cigarettes to the animals.

It is unlawful for goldfish to ride on a Seattle, Washington, bus unless they lie still.

In Berkeley, California, you cannot whistle for your lost canary before seven o'clock in the morn-ing.

In Vermont, painting a horse is illegal.

Candidates for public office in Kansas are not allowed to give away cigars on election day.

In Natchez, Mississippi, it is against the law for elephants to drink beer.

In Oak Park, Illinois, the law restricts the making of doughnuts to no more than one hundred per person in one day.

In Florida, you can be sent to jail for luring your neighbor's cook away to work for you.

In Minnesota, women are forbidden from appearing on the street dressed up as Santa Claus.

A judge in Michigan decided that a woman's hair is the property of her husband.

In Prichard, Alabama, men are required by law to wear tops to their bathing suits.

It is illegal to carry bees in your hat in the streets of Lawrence, Kansas.

In Cleveland, Ohio, you are not allowed to kill your neighbor's chickens unless you have written permission from a majority of the residents within five hundred feet.

An ordinance was passed in Fairbanks, Alaska, to keep moose off the sidewalks.

Many Harvard undergraduates are breaking an old law of Cambridge, Massachusetts, which banned long hair among students.

It is a violation of the laws of Waterville, Maine, to blow your nose in public.

Women jurors in Mexico, Missouri, cannot knit while they are in court.

In Utah, the law requires that daylight be seen between two dancing partners.

In Nebraska, it is illegal for a woman to wave her daughter's hair without a state license.

In Logansport, Indiana, it is illegal to wheel a baby carriage along the sidewalk.

It is illegal to mispronounce the name of the city of Joliet, Illinois.

In Massachusetts, men are not permitted in women's hairdressing salons for hair tinting or waving.

In White Cloud, Kansas, it is illegal to break out of jail.

In New York State it is illegal to pawn an American flag.

To drown rats in the city's sewer system, the city clerk of Berkeley, California, was empowered to order all bathtubs in the city to be filled, and then unplugged all at once.

Illinois law requires all healthy males between twenty-one and fifty years old to work in the streets two days each year.

Railroad cars left standing in the street in Baltimore, Maryland, must be properly chained.

In old Connecticut, only authorized clergymen could cross the river on Sunday.

In Macon, Georgia, for a man to put his arm around a woman, he must have a legal excuse or reason.

A person can be charged with first-degree murder in Oklahoma for killing an animal "with malicious intent."

In Connecticut, luring bees away from their owner is an illegal act.

Sleeping on the floor of the Kentucky State House is prohibited.

Taxicabs in Youngstown, Ohio, are not allowed to carry passengers on the roof.

Salt Lake City, Utah, has a law against carrying an unwrapped ukelele on the street.

In Colorado Springs, Colorado, the law upholds a dog's right to one bite.

Indiana has a law against taking a bath in the wintertime.